Little
Pebble™

Our Amazing Sen[ses]

Our Noses Can
Smell

by Jodi Wheeler-Toppen

CAPSTONE PRESS
a capstone imprint

Little Pebble is published by Capstone Press,
1710 Roe Crest Drive, North Mankato, Minnesota 56003
www.mycapstone.com

Library of Congress Cataloging-in-Publication Data
Names: Wheeler-Toppen, Jodi, author.
Title: Our noses can smell / by Jodi Wheeler-Toppen.
Description: North Mankato, Minnesota : Capstone Press, [2018] | Series: Our
    amazing senses | Audience: Age 4-7. | Audience: K to grade 3. | Includes
    bibliographical references and index.
Identifiers: LCCN 2017005232 (print) | LCCN 2017006588 (ebook)
ISBN 9781515767114 (library binding)
ISBN 9781515767176 (paperback)
ISBN 9781515767220 (eBook PDF)
Subjects: LCSH: Smell—Juvenile literature. | Nose—Juvenile literature. |
    Senses and sensation—Juvenile literature.
Classification: LCC QP458 .W44 2018 (print) | LCC QP458 (ebook) | DDC
    612.8/6—dc23
LC record available at https://lccn.loc.gov/2017005232

Editorial Credits

Abby Colich, editor; Juliette Peters, designer; Wanda Winch, media researcher;
Tori Abraham, production specialist

Photo Credits

iStockphoto: asiseeit, 7; Science Source: John M. Daugherty, 11; Shutterstock: agsandrew, motion design element, Blend Images, 1, DenisFilm, 17, goa novi, 9, Gundam_Ai, 19, Philippe Put, 21, Sheila Fitzgerald, 13, tommaso79, 5, viavetal, cover; Thinkstock: Stockbyte/ George Doyle, 15

Printed in the United States   6012

Table of Contents

A Good Smell

Dad is baking.

Ooh! It smells so good.

What is it?

In Your Nose

Smell moves in the air.

It goes in your nose holes.

They are called nostrils.

Your nose is like a cave.

It starts at your nostrils.

It goes to your throat.

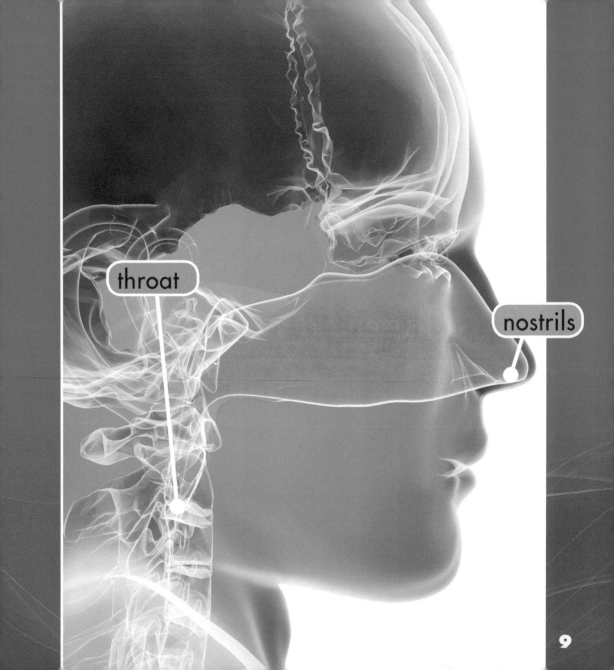

throat

nostrils

Your nose has cells.

Smell hits the cells.

The cells send a signal.

It goes to your brain.

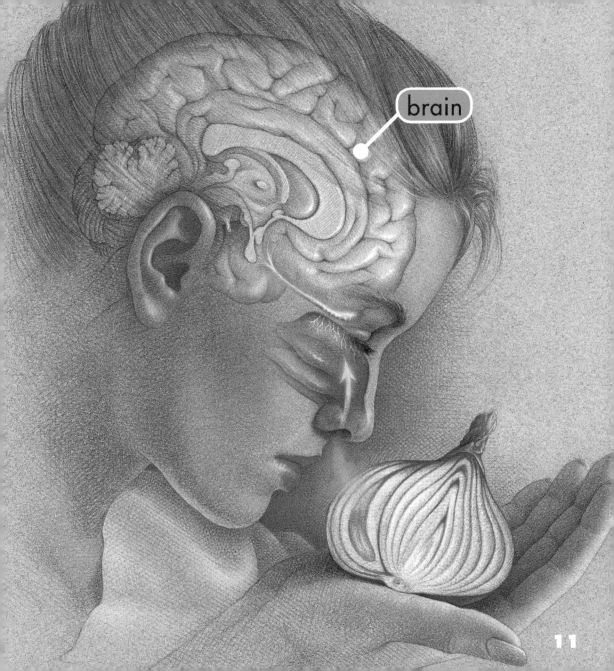

brain

Your brain knows the smell.

Ah ha! It is cake. **Yum!**

We Use Smell

Hold your nose.

Take a bite. **Gulp!**

Where did the taste go?

Smell and taste work together. You need smell to taste.

Eww! The milk is stinky.

Uh oh! Stop! Don't drink it.

Smell keeps you safe.

Yuck! The trash is icky.

Your nose smells bad things.

Mmm. A flower is a good smell.

Your nose smells the good too.

Glossary

brain—the organ inside your head that controls your movements, thoughts, and feelings

cave—a large hole underground or in the side of a hill or cliff

cell—the smallest unit of a living thing

nostril—openings in the nose used to breathe and smell

signal—a message between the brain and the senses

Read More

Appleby, Alex. *What I Smell.* My Five Senses. New York: Gareth Stevens Publishing, 2014.

Murray, Julie. *I Can Smell.* Senses. Minneapolis, Minn.: Abdo Kids, 2016.

Rustad, Martha E.H. *Smelling.* Senses in My World. Minneapolis, Minn.: Bullfrog Books, 2015.

Internet Sites

Use FactHound to find Internet sites related to this book.

Visit *www.facthound.com*
Type in this code: 9781515767114

Check out projects, games and lots more at
www.capstonekids.com

Critical Thinking Questions

1. What are your nose holes called?

2. Use the glossary to define *cave*. Then look at page 9. How is the nose like a cave?

3. Reread page 18. Think of another way smell keeps you safe.

Index